Paper chains

Leisure Crafts 71

G000293363

SEARCH PRESS
London & New York

Introduction

Paperchain making is an enjoyable hobby for the long winter evenings leading up to Christmas, but also for any time before a festive or special occasion. This book shows you how to make original and colourful paper chains at a fraction of the cost of ready-made decorations.

If you make them carefully and store them neatly after use, there is no reason why your paper chains should not last for any number of party occasions at home, college or place of work.

None of the paper chains described in this book is really difficult to make, but if you want to involve very young children, or to begin with something really simple, turn to page 26 and make the simple chains described there.

After making up the patterns in this book you should be able to introduce your own variations on the designs, and to enjoy the use of unique decorations.

A simple garland with greenery.

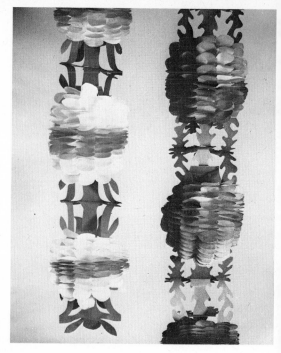

Blossom sections with pull-out paper vines.

Materials

Tissue paper. A large range of colours is available, so you are not restricted to the colours used here.

Cartridge or pastel paper

Thin card

Glue. The best glues for this purpose are those which are sold in 'lipstick-type' containers. Some glues will soak through several layers of tissue paper and ruin your chains, and others will take too long to dry. If in doubt about the suitability of a glue, experiment with scraps of tissue paper before applying it to your paper chains.

Sharp scissors

Needle and thread or stapler

fig. 1

The first four paper chain patterns are based on the template shown in its actual size in fig. 1. Trace the drawing and, with carbon paper under your tracing, transfer it to a piece of thin card which you then cut out. The use of a template saves time and helps you to cut your tissue shapes to the same size.

When working out a template of your own design (should you decide to introduce your own variations on those shown here), remember that your shapes should have an even number of petals or lobes.

Simple floral garlands

Use the template (fig. 1) on page 3 to cut out a number of tissue shapes in the colour of your choice. Take the first of these tissue shapes and glue at the points marked *A* in fig. 2. Place a second shape on top and glue it at the points marked *B*. Place a third tissue shape on top and glue it at the points marked *A*. Glue alternate sheets in this way until you have a garland of the required length.

The more carefully you apply the glue and accurately position the tissue sheets, the better the final result.

Use the template as a guide to cut out two pieces of thin card for supports at the beginning and end of your garland. Trim them slightly smaller than the tissue paper so that they give the necessary stability without being noticeable. Fold the card in half and cut tabs at the centre for use when fastening the garland to a wall or ceiling (fig. 3).

fig. 3

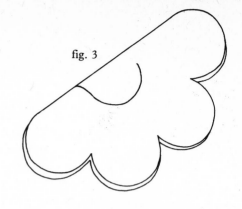

Opposite: *a simple floral garland that uses the template in fig. 1.*
Below: *detail of the simple floral garland.*

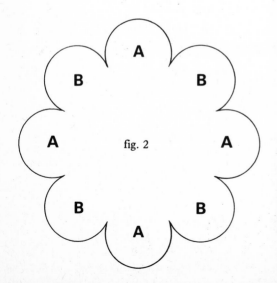

fig. 2

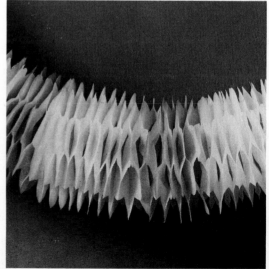

4

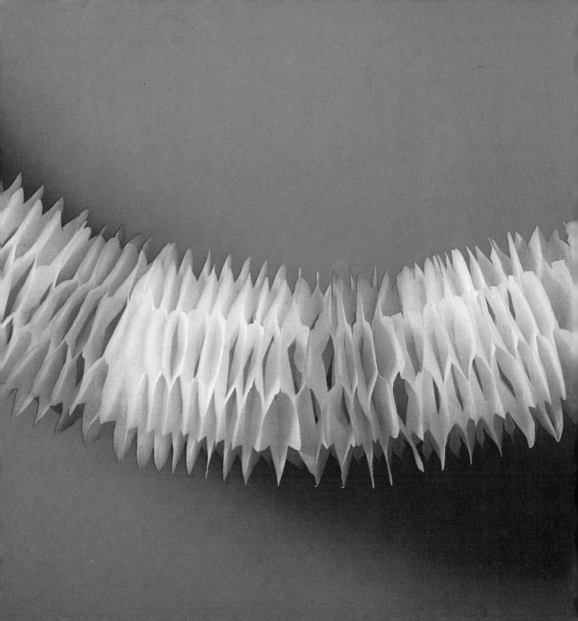

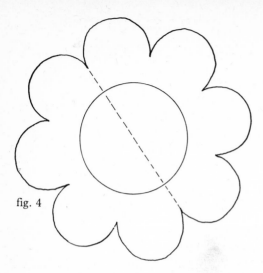

fig. 4

Greenery with alternating blossoms

For this example you will need to prepare some 'blossoms' before assembling the garland. Take four sheets of tissue which have been cut to the template shape in fig. 1. Glue the tissue sheets, alternating at points *A* and *B* shown in fig. 5. When you have glued the fourth sheet, fold it over, and continue gluing and folding until all four sheets are folded as shown in fig. 6.

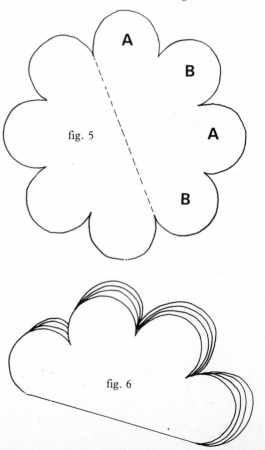

Greenery garlands

This is a quicker method of producing long lengths of garlands, and can be combined with the floral garlands just described.

Use the template in fig. 1 to cut shapes from green tissue paper. Fold the tissue shapes in half and cut a semi-circle from the centre so that it will form a complete circle when the shapes are opened out (fig. 4).

Apply small dabs of glue in the same order as was given for floral garlands, but apply it very carefully as these tissue paper shapes are more fragile. To avoid the risk of tearing, position your thumb and forefinger on either side of the point being glued.

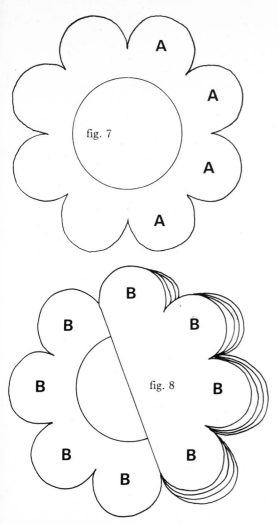

fig. 7

fig. 8

Prepare as many of these blossom sections as you think you need, then cut some green tissue paper, again following the template shown in fig. 1, and remove the centres as shown in fig. 4.

Whichever number you decide to use, it is best to count your cut tissue paper shapes into piles before you start gluing, otherwise you are likely to lose count and your finished garland will appear uneven.

Glue the greenery cut-outs alternately at points A and B (fig. 3), but when you reach the final sheet in the greenery section, glue it at the points marked A in fig. 7, and attach your first blossom section at these points. When the blossom section is firmly attached, apply glue to it at the eight points marked B in fig. 8, and attach the first sheet of your next section of greenery.

Carry on adding the same number of greenery cut-outs as before, and alternate with blossom sections until you have a garland of the required length.

A garland of twining blossom.

This garland uses only two sheets of tissue paper for each blossom, with one sheet of greenery between each blossom section. Instead of blossoms being placed on alternate sides, as in the last example, they will now move round one place each time.

Prepare a number of blossom sections as you did for the last example, but using only two sheets of tissue paper for each. Have ready some greenery tissues with cut-out centres.

Take one sheet of greenery and glue it at the four points marked A in fig. 9. Attach the first blossom section to it and then apply glue on the other side of the blossom section at the two points marked A in fig. 10. Now attach the second sheet of greenery, and when it is in position, put a dab of glue at the four points marked B in fig. 11. Attach the second blossom section so that it moves one section clockwise, and apply glue at the points marked B in fig. 12 ready to take the next sheet of greenery.

Continue working in this way, gluing alternately at A and B, and moving the blossom sections round one place clockwise each time.

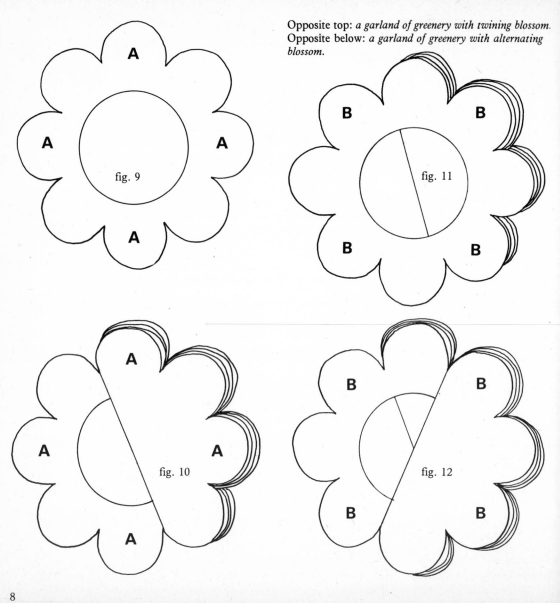

Opposite top: *a garland of greenery with twining blossom.*
Opposite below: *a garland of greenery with alternating blossom.*

A

A

A

fig. 9

A

B

B

fig. 11

B

B

A

A

fig. 10

A

A

B

B

fig. 12

B

B

Christmas tree ornaments

To make the attractive tree decorations shown on page 12 you need a thin piece of card and thirty sheets of tissue paper each cut in circles of 75 mm (3 in.) diameter (fig. 13).

Fastening the tissue paper sheets

Fold the sheets and the card exactly in half to find the centre line. Fasten the tissues and card together either by sewing or by using staples along the centre line. Use a simple 'three-hole' bookbinding stitch (fig. 14) for sewing. Leave an inch or two of thread hanging from the centre and, after pulling the needle through the third hole, pass it under the first stitch and tie the two ends of thread together (fig. 15).

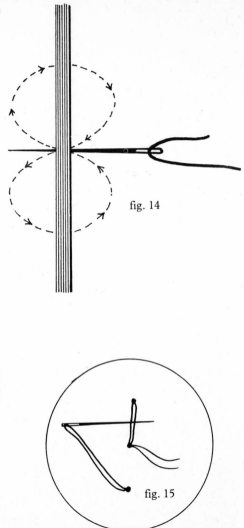

fig. 14

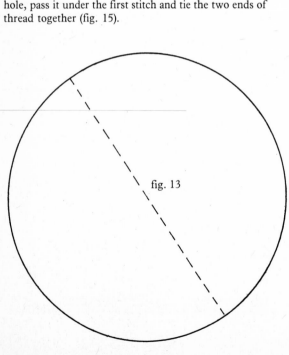

fig. 13

fig. 15

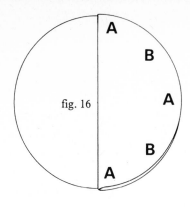

fig. 16

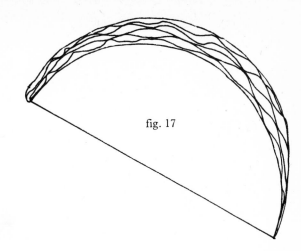

fig. 17

Gluing the leaves

With the tissue paper side laying face downwards, fold the card back on itself. Pick up the first tissue paper sheet and glue it securely to the card. Glue the second sheet of tissue paper to the first at the points marked *A* in fig. 16. Glue the third tissue paper sheet to the second at the points marked *B* in fig. 16; the fourth at *A;* the fifth at *B;* and so on, until you reach the final sheet.

Turn the 'book' over and glue the other halves of the tissue paper circles in the same way. This time, when you reach the final sheet, glue it at both points *A* and *B* and fold the card to meet it so that the two are attached together (fig. 17).

Note: When applying glue to these open-out shapes, try to keep the glue well within the edge of the tissue paper shapes, otherwise you will find them difficult to open out. Always give the glue plenty of time to set before attempting to open out the shape. Even so, you may still find one or two points which will need to be re-glued.

To complete your decoration, fasten a piece of thread at the back of the card for hanging and use a paper-clip over the folded card to keep the shape opened out.

Detail of Christmas tree ornaments shown on page 12.

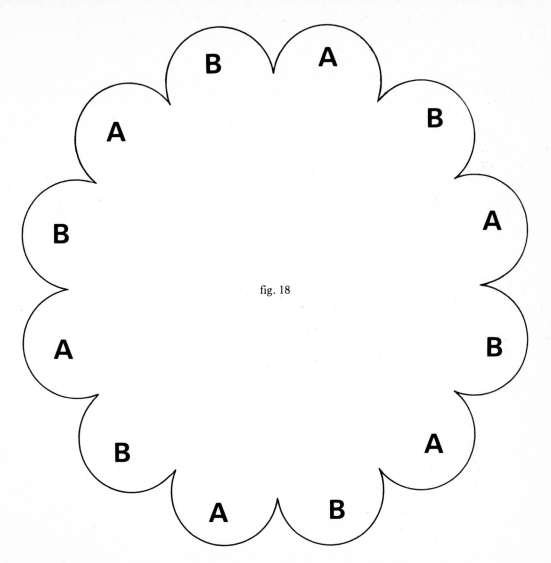

fig. 18

Opposite: *Christmas tree ornaments.*

Floral garland with pull-out paper vine

The floral sections for this example, pictured on page 16, are made in exactly the same way as those in the simple floral garlands, except that the tissue paper is cut to a larger size.

Prepare some flower sections using the template shown in fig. 18, and glue alternate *A* and *B* petals as previously described.

Twenty-eight leaves of tissue paper were used for each flower section in the example.

Making the paper vine

To make the vine you need some thicker paper; pastel or cartridge paper is ideal, but first make a template in thin card from the shape shown in fig. 19.

Place the template on a piece of the green pastel or cartridge paper which has been folded into quarters (fig. 20). Cut round the template and along the inner four lines and open it out to form the shape shown in fig. 21.

fig. 20

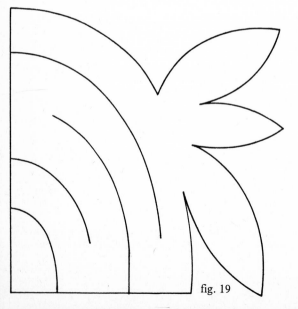

fig. 19

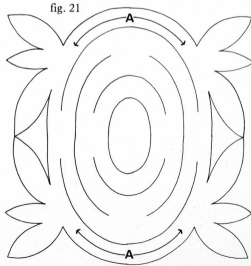

fig. 21

A

A

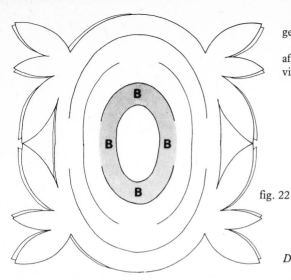

Prepare a number of these 'vines' and glue them together in pairs along the parts marked *A*.

Attach the flower sections between two pairs of vines after you have applied glue on the inner edges of the vines at the point marked *B* in fig. 22.

fig. 22

Detail of floral garland with pull-out paper vine.

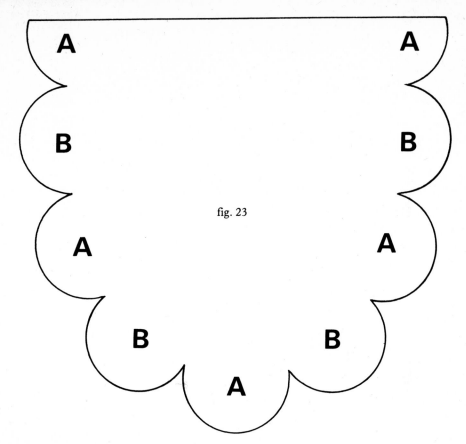

fig. 23

Page 16: *a floral garland with pull-out paper vines using the templates in figs. 18 and 19.*

Blossom sections with pull-out paper vines

The blossom sections in this example are similar to those used in the alternating blossom garland described on page 6.

Place the template shown in fig. 23 on folded sheets of tissue paper so that the leaves are doubled as shown in fig. 24. If you prefer, you can cut them out individually and glue them in pairs along the top edge.

In the example shown on page 21 twelve double leaves were used for each blossom section, and alternate lobes were glued together as in all previous examples.

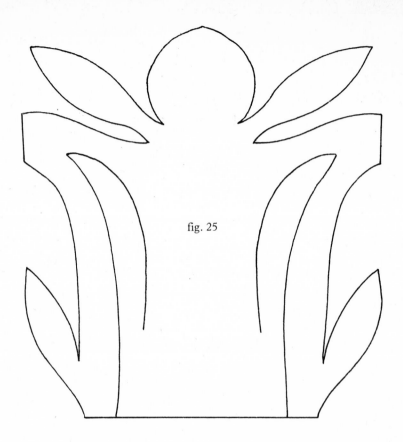

fig. 25

Making the vine

Fold a sheet of cartridge or pastel paper in half. Place the straight edge of the template shown in fig. 25 along the fold, and cut out the shape as shown in fig. 26. Prepare a number of these shapes since you will need two for every section of blossom.

Open out the vine shapes and glue at the points marked *A* in fig. 27, making sure that you glue up as far as the dotted line in the diagram. Fold the two halves of the vine shape together again, and press together to ensure that they are firmly attached. These parts of the vine will pull out in a straight line, with the blossom hanging between them.

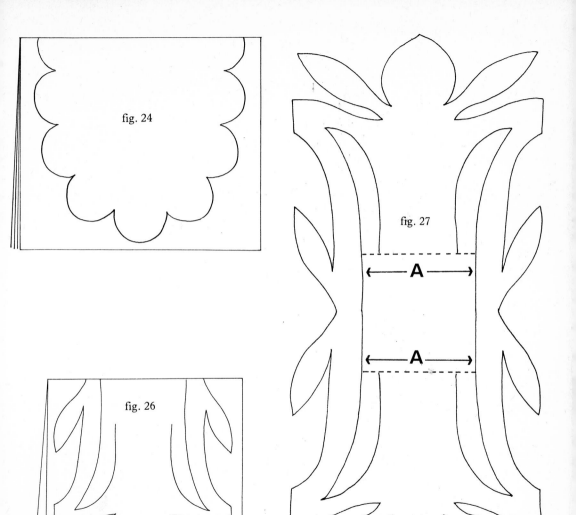

fig. 24

fig. 26

fig. 27

A

A

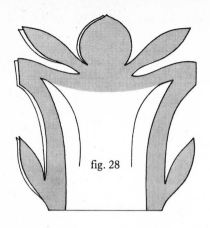

fig. 28

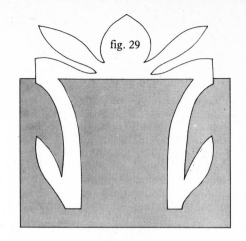

fig. 29

Opposite: blossom sections with pull-out paper vines.

Detail of a blossom section with pull-out paper vine.

Gluing the blossom and vine together

Take one of the completed vine sections and apply glue to one side on the area indicated by shading in fig. 28. To do this accurately, you should either fold back the centre vine leaves or mask them with a piece of scrap paper (fig. 29).

Place the first blossom section in the position indicated in fig. 30.

Glue another vine section in the same way as the first (fig. 28), and attach this on the opposite side of the blossom so that the two vine patterns meet at the top where they project over the blossom.

Prepare each of your blossom sections with a vine on either side, then you are ready to join all the sections together.

To join the sections, glue the outer parts of a vine following the shaded area shown in fig. 31 and attach the next completed section to it.

If you wish, an alternative vine pattern may be used, and a template for the vine shown in the photograph on page 21 is shown in fig. 32.

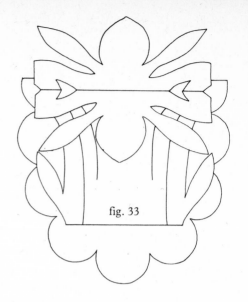

fig. 30

fig. 33

fig. 31

Paper vines with alternating blossom

The blossom and vine sections here are made up in exactly the same way as for the previous example. The only difference occurs when gluing the sections together.

Apply glue to the first section as shown in fig. 31.

Take the second completed section and fold back the outer part of the vine as shown in fig. 33. The part you have folded back should now be glued to the first section.

Repeat this procedure on the opposite side of the section which should then be glued to the third section in the same way.

Continue alternating blossom sections in this way until your garland is of the required length.

This paper chain is shown on the cover.

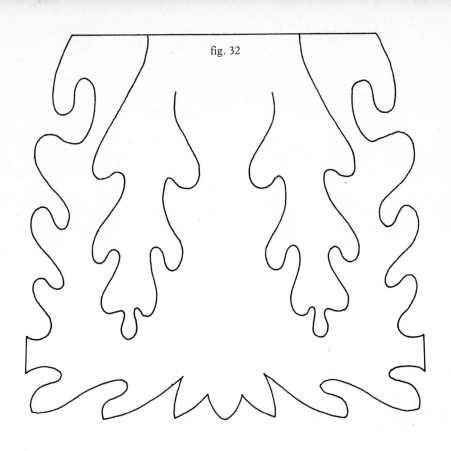

fig. 32

Page 24, top: *simple paperchains*. Below: *paperchains with hanging blossom.*

Page 25: *traditional pull-out paper garlands.*

23

Simple paper chains

This is a very quick way of producing lengths of decoration, and it is simple enough for a child to enjoy.

Prepare a number of tissue sheets about 160 × 45 mm (6¼ × 1¾ in.) and glue them according to the gluing pattern shown in fig. 34: the first sheet at *A*, the second at *B*, the third at *A*, and so on.

You can leave the edges plain, or for a more interesting effect, scallop the edges before gluing. A template for scalloping is shown in fig. 34.

Paper chains with hanging blossom

Cut a number of tissue shapes from the scallop pattern shown in fig. 34. You can use two colours for the chain – I used green and blue, and a third colour for the blossom, which I made in pink.

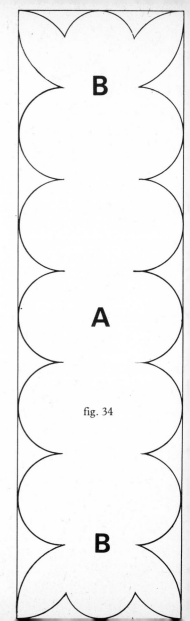

fig. 34

fig. 35

fig. 36

fig. 37

fig. 38

Making the blossom sections

Use five tissue paper sheets for each section. The gluing pattern is shown in fig. 35. Glue the first sheet at *A*, the second at *B*, the third at *A*, and so on until you reach the fifth sheet. After gluing the fifth sheet, fold all the sheets in half as shown in fig. 36.

Fixing the chain and blossom together

The use of two colours for the chain will help you keep count when placing your blossom sections. I fixed mine between two blue tissue paper cut-outs, with two green tissues on either side.

Following the gluing pattern shown in fig. 34, glue the first (green) sheet at *A*, and attach the second (green) sheet which should be glued at *B*. Attach the third (blue) sheet and glue it at A, but to make the blossom section spread out, also glue it at *C* (fig. 37).

Attach the blossom section in position (fig. 38), and glue it at points *A* and *C* ready to take the next piece of chain tissue (blue). Glue the chain tissue at *B* and add two more green tissues as before.

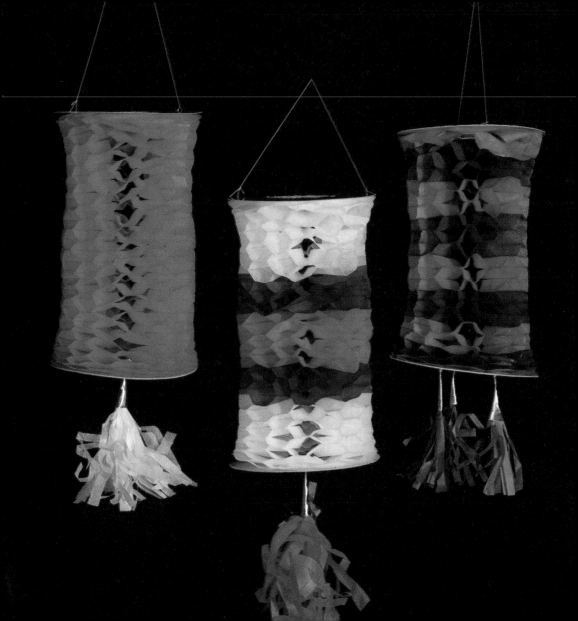

Hanging lanterns

You can make lanterns following the same principle as for the simple floral garlands at the beginning of the book, but to make them more solid I have used more gluing points.

Prepare the tissue paper cut-outs – you will need about thirty for each lantern. I have used plain circles, but the shape can be varied as you wish.

When you are ready to start gluing, you will find it helpful to draw a circle the same size as your cut-out tissues on a separate sheet of paper, marking the eight gluing points for the first sheet as shown in fig. 39. Tissue sheets should be glued alternately, first at points *A,* then at points *B,* and so on, as in previous examples.

When all thirty sheets have been glued, trim the edges for a neat finish. Cut a circle from the centre of the completed glued shapes before gluing the bottom tissue sheet to a circular cardboard base cut to the same size as the tissue paper sheets.

Opposite: *hanging lanterns.*

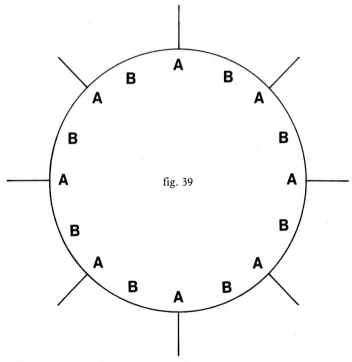

fig. 39

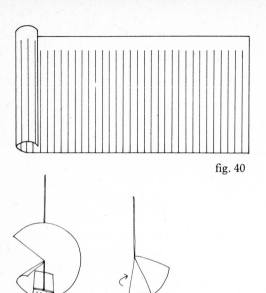

fig. 40

fig. 41

Traditional pull-out paper garlands

These are quite quick and easy to make and you will soon find that you have a long length of chain ready for hanging.

Cut a number of tissue paper circles and cut two circles from thin card for the ends.

Fold about ten tissue paper circles in half, and then in half again. Make two cuts in them as shown in fig. 42. Treat all the leaves in the same way, but don't try to fold and cut too many at one time − ten leaves is about the right number.

Gluing is very simple. Put a dab of glue in the middle of one of the cardboard ends and place the first tissue paper sheet on it. Put two dabs of glue on the first sheet at the points marked *B* in fig. 43 and attach the second tissue paper sheet. Continue gluing alternate sheets at points *A* and *B* until you have finished.

Note: Because there are several cuts in the tissue paper leaves you will find that you have to support the tissue paper by placing fingers on either side of the point being glued to prevent tearing the delicate shapes.

Make tassels from a rectangular tissue paper sheet which should be cut as shown in fig. 40 and then rolled round a pencil or knitting needle. Secure the uncut edge with thread leaving an end of thread long enough to stitch the tassel to the lantern. Decorate the top of the tassel with a small circular piece of tinfoil wrapped round the end after a segment has been cut out as shown in fig. 41.

Finally, glue a circle of card with a cut-out centre to the top of the lantern and attach a thread for hanging.

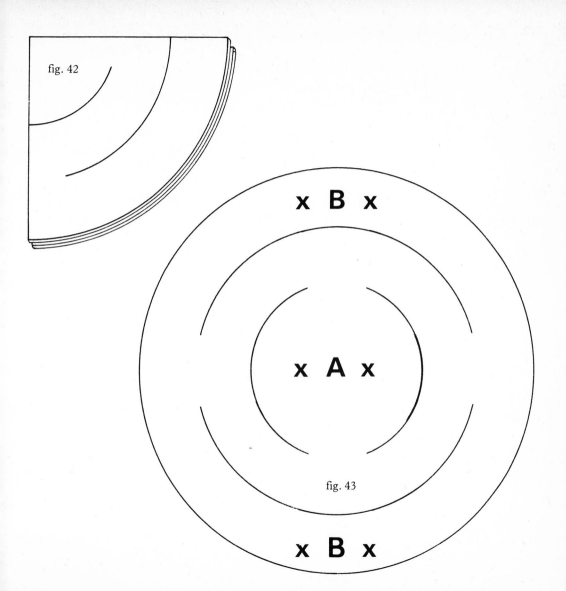

fig. 42

x B x

x A x

fig. 43

x B x

Acknowledgements

Text and diagrams by Bill Leeson

Photographs by Search Press Studios

Text, illustrations, arrangement and typography copyright © Search Press Limited 1979

First published in Great Britain in 1979 by Search Press Limited, 2-10 Jerdan Place, London SW6 5PT

ISBN 0 85532 482 1

Printed in England by Garrod and Lofthouse Limited